I0409620

# THE UNRAVELING
# OF
# AMERICA
# THE OBAMA
# ADMINISTRATION
# A TRILOGY IN
# "F"

## 1: FANTASY

## 2: FACT

## 3: FUTURE

## <u>INTRODUCTION</u>

I would never have thought I would write anything of this nature,or even to have taken interest, but, here it is:

My family did not have much interest in politics, certainly, my peers through high school did not have interest. Politics came to me at the age of 19, in 1960 when the magic of Camelot piqued my interest

JFK was such a force that his entire presence magnetized you to be connected to him in any way possible. His words were eloquent, mostly unscripted. They were spoken in unison with his posture, movement, facial expression, and eye twinkling. Wrapping every encounter into his entire persona. To me he was and still is an intellectual Frank Sinatra

During the Democratic convention of 1959 and the primaries that preceded, I watched as Lyndon Johnson emerged as Kennedy's pick for VP. My impression of Johnson was that he was the strongest most manipulative politician of his time. (The current TV series House of Cards has Kevin Spacey playing a similar politician.)

I was so focused on who Johnson was that I actually thought he could have orchestrated the assassination of President Kennedy. However after Johnson was sworn in as President he used his power to try to create many humanitarian and Civil Rights programs.

## **INTRODUCTION**

His progress was hampered by the toll that the Vietnam war took upon him, Lyndon Baines Johnson entered the office with vim, vigor and good intentions. He left a worn, aged, beaten man, all contributing factors to his early demise.

Richard Nixon had the intelligence and ability to have accomplished a lot more than he did, especially in international affairs. But, Mr Nixon was a flawed man with a tremendous insecurity problem which led to his Presidential demise

Gerald Ford and Jimmy Carter, occupied the White House, but as far as I saw it, did not have any of the abilities required for leadership.

Ronald Reagan, did not concern himself with his party base. He focused on the major problems that needed to be corrected and through self assurance, good leadership qualities, and the ability to select the proper advisers, he had a very successful tenure

George H.W. Bush, A well-rounded family man, brought intelligence, experience, and flawless values to the White house. He embodied the lifestyle of a pure Gentleman. Had he been reelected, his legacy of accomplishments would have loomed large.

Bill Clinton, a master of leadership, bright and unafraid, had the ability to appoint all the right people in the right places and soared as a great President, in spite of his sexual immaturity.

## **INTRODUCTION**

George W. Bush  faced an unprecedented disaster: the terrorist attacks of 9/11. He faced this atrocity with composed decisiveness and displayed to the world that no one can inflict harm upon America without major consequence.

Mr. Bush had the same qualities as his father, but because he spoke off the cuff and with a down-home style he was disrespected by the pseudo sophisticate, and the Monday morning quarterback,.

The bashing he received by the relentless vitriol of Democrats in every walk of life was disrespectfully unwarranted. It is my opinion that History will vindicate him.

The 2008 Presidential campaign, did not even have to be negotiated, as Obama, buoyed by a very astute campaign committee left the gate in front and never looked back

I felt he should run as Vice President on the ticket with Hillary for President. Eight years later he would be a candidate for President with Washington DC, White House and Clinton-ian experience in his resume.

I was of the opinion that because of his flirtations with radicals and questionable characters. Because of his lack of experience in leadership of anything, he was not yet qualified to be President.

## INTRODUCTION

Some of the radical and questionable characters are as follows:

**Tony Rezko** : a former engineer, real estate developer, and businessman who is now in prison for wire fraud, bribery, money laundering, and attempted extortion as a result of a federal investigation known as "Operation Board Games".

Mr. Rezko's businesses were in the district that Barack Obama represented when he was a State Senator for Illinois. Accusations have been made concerning contributions made to the Obama campaign. There is also evidence that the house Barack Obama purchased after becoming a U.S. Senator was improperly obtained from Mr. Rezko.

**Reverend Wright** In documented speeches, Rev. Wright proclaimed the following:" The government gives them [African Americans] the drugs, builds bigger prisons, passes a three-strike law and then wants us to sing 'God Bless America.' No, no, no, God damn America, that's in the Bible for killing innocent people. God damn America for treating our citizens as less than human. God damn America for as long as she acts like she is God and she is supreme."

After September 11, 2001, he said: "We have supported state terrorism against the Palestinians and black South Africans and now we are indignant because the stuff we have done overseas is now brought right back into our own front yards. America's chickens are coming home to roost."

## INTRODUCTION

"It just came to me within the past few weeks, y'all, why so many folks are hating on Barack Obama. He doesn't fit the model. He ain't white, he ain't rich, and he ain't privileged. Hillary fits the mold. Europeans fit the mold, Giuliani fits the mold. Rich white men fit the mold. Hillary never had a cab whiz past her and not pick her up because her skin was the wrong color. Hillary never had to worry about being pulled over in her car as a black man driving in the wrong…

"I am sick of Negroes who just do not get it. Hillary was not a black boy raised in a single parent home, Barack was. Barack knows what it means to be a black man living in a country and a culture that is controlled by rich white people. Hillary can never know that. Hillary ain't never been called a nigger. Hillary has never had her people defined as non-persons."

He went on to say Bill Clinton "did the same thing to us that he did to Monica Lewinsky."

"We bombed Hiroshima. We bombed Nagasaki and we nuked far more than the thousands in New York and the Pentagon and we never batted an eye."

"America is still the No. 1 killer in the world. ... We are deeply involved in the importing of drugs, the exporting of guns and the training of professional killers. ..."

### .  **INTRODUCTION**

"We believe in white supremacy and black inferiority and believe it more than we believe in God. ... We supported Zionism shamelessly while ignoring the Palestinians and branding anybody who spoke out against it as being anti-Semitic. ... We started the AIDS virus. ... We are only able to maintain our level of living by making sure that Third World people live in grinding poverty."

Barack Obama began attending Reverend Wrights Church (TUCC) in 1988 after moving to Chicago to become a community organizer.

After graduating from Harvard Law School and returning to Chicago, Barack became a member of Trinity in 1992. In his 1995 memoir "Dreams from my Father" Barack states that Reverend Wright impressed him as he spoke of "the audacity of hope" in times of suffering.

Over the next decade, Reverend Wright would marry Barack and Michelle Obama, bless their children, and provide spiritual support for Senator Obama while Senator Obama would draw on the phrase "The Audacity of Hope" as the title to his next book.

Senator Obama gave a speech at TUCC near the beginning of his Presidential campaign and when questioned about his relationship with Reverend Wright on MSNBC, Mr. Obama made the following statement:

## INTRODUCTION

"I have known him 17 years. He helped bring me to Jesus and helped bring me to church. He and I have a relationship; he's like an uncle who talked to me, not about political things and social views, but faith and God and family."

**Bill Ayers** Radical activist and co-founder of revolutionary group the Weather Underground. The relationship between Ayers and Obama first became an issue in the 2008 election after journalist George Stephanopoulos mentioned it. Later, Republican vice-Presidential candidate Sarah Palin accused Obama of "palling around with a terrorist."

.

Below is a fairly comprehensive list of activities and Bombing convictions of Bill Ayers.

October 1969 – Bombing of Haymarket Police Statue in Chicago.

The "Days of Rage" riots occur in Chicago in which 287 Weatherman members from throughout the country were arrested and a large amount of property damage was done.

December 1969 – Bombing of several Chicago Police cars.

January 1970  Weathermen hold a "War Council" meeting in Flint, MI where they finalize their plans to submerge into an underground status.

**INTRODUCTION**

February 1970 – Bombing of several police vehicles in Berkeley, CA;

February 1970: Bombing of the San Francisco Police Department, killing one officer and injuring a number of other policemen.

March 1970 – Bombing in the 13th Police District of the Detroit, MI.

1970 "Bomb factory" located in New York's Greenwich Village accidentally explodes. WUO members die. The bomb was intended to be planted at a non-commissioned officer's dance at Fort Dix, NJ. The bomb was packed with nails to inflict maximum casualties upon detonation.

1970 Chicago Police discover a WUO "bomb factory" on Chicago's north side.

1970 A subsequent discovery of a WUO "weapons cache" in an apartment on the south side Chicago. Several days later WUO activity in the city ends.

May 1970 – Bombing of The National Guard in Washington,D.C.

May 1970 The WUO under (Ayers wife) Bernardine Dohrn's name releases its "Declaration of a State of War"communique.

June 1970 – The WUO sends a letter claiming credit for Bombing of the San Francisco Hall of Justice;

## **INTRODUCTION**

1970  Bombing of the New York City Police Headquarters.

July 1970 – Bombing of The Presidio army base in San Francisco.

September 1970 – The WUO helps Dr. Timothy Leary escape from the California Men's Colony prison.

October 1970 – Bombing of Marin County, CA courthouse;

1970  Bombing of Queens, NY traffic court building;

1971  Bombing of The Harvard Center for International Affairs.

March 1971 – Bombing of the United States Capitol in Washington, DC.

April 1971 – abandoned WUO "bomb factory" discovered in San Francisco.

August 1971 – Bombing of the Office of California Prisons.

September 1971 – Bombing New York Department of Corrections in Albany, NY.

## **INTRODUCTION**

October 1971 – Bombing of William Bundy's office in the MIT research center, Boston, MA.

May 1972–Bombing of The Pentagon;

June 1972-Bombing of the 103rd Police Precinct in New York City.

September 1973 – Bombing of ITT headquarters in New York and Rome, Italy.

March 1974 – Bombing of Health, Education and Welfare offices in San-Francisco

May 1974 – Bombing of The Office of the California Attorney General.

June 1974 – Bombing of the headquarters of Gulf Oil in Pittsburgh.

September 1974 – Bombing of Anaconda Corporation (Rockefeller Corporation).

January 1975 – Bombing of the State Department in Washington, DC.

June 1975 – Bombing of Banco de Ponce (a Puerto Rican bank) in New York.

## **INTRODUCTION**

September 1975 – Bombing of the Kennecott Corporation.

October 1981 – Brinks robbery in which several members of the Weather Underground stole over $1 million from a Brinks armored car near Nyack, NY. The robbers murdered two police officers and one Brinks guard. Several others were wounded.

In 1981 after all the murders and devastation perpetrated on innocent people, David Horowitz, Interviewed Bill Ayers who said the following:

"I am Guilty as hell. Free as a bird. America is a great country."

September 11, 2001  Ayers is quoted in a New York Times article:

"I don't regret setting bombs. I feel we didn't do enough."

The terrorizing history of Mr Ayers and his wife goes way beyond the terror above. You have to more then wonder what kind of person would associate with them ?

As Obama's Presidential bid gained steam it became apparent that his campaign operators were more adept in modern technology than Hillary Clinton and John McCain

## **INTRODUCTION**

With the addition of a focus on getting their voters out to the Polls, the campaign became like a snowball rolling down a mountain. That momentum took him over the finish line in the primary and Presidential election.

As an Independent, I would have voted for a Clinton/Obama ticket over McCain. Aside from her own competence Hillary would have the ability to council a former highly regarded President in her husband. But, there was no individual or combination of individuals that could have beaten Obama at this point.

So now you have it Barack Obama.President Elect, of the United States of America, and beloved everywhere including abroad.

As time passed, his leadership skills and political views left me uncomfortable. I thought there were missteps and he was moving in a direction that we the people opposed. I started to write notes, to refer to at some point, as I feared there was something going wrong. I was not sure whether it was a push toward Socialism, personal incompetence by Barack, or intentional misleading.

After years of these feelings and the reelection of President Obama, I said to myself, 'what a shame. He had the confidence of the whole world in his hands. He could have done monumental things.'

## **INTRODUCTION**

I decided to create my opinion of what these things could be. The first, of my trilogy

"Fantasy,"

The second; ,

 "Fact,"

The third

 "Future"

## FANTASY

Historically unprecedented, President Elect Obama addressed the nation on the day after his victory. He proclaimed that the myriad of problems facing our country need to be addressed in a swift but articulate manner.

Cabinet member's must be selected on the basis of their expertise that will enable them to successfully chair a committee formed to correct one of our many crisis. That person must be able to devote his full time and attention to the matters at hand.

The President Elect went on to say that former presidents were pressured to select their cabinets based on political debt or cronyism. The problems facing us require the sacrifice and focus of the most capable advisers available working in bipartisanship.

Therefore at 10 a.m. that very morning President Elect Obama held a conference call with former Presidents Bill Clinton and George W. Bush, former Secretary of State Henry Kissinger, renowned scholar Charles Krauthammer, and General Colin Powell. Obama asked if they would serve on an advisory board to help select the cabinet members, and to serve as on-going advisers to the President

## FANTASY

Honored and anxious, the five dignitaries, made the decision to form a nine member board. The additional members were to be selected by the five already appointed. The advisory board would meet once per week. In order to fulfill his campaign promise to have the most transparent administration in history.The minutes would be posted immediately on the committee's website

This historical event ingratiated the President Elect to the hearts and minds of a struggling nation and the world.

Within the next four weeks, the most brilliant minds and highly experienced leaders in their fields where submitted to the President Elect for his approval. The President's cabinet and advisory board were set in place.

The inauguration of America's first black President and First Family was watched and applauded throughout the world.

For each area of crisis a committee was formed comprising House and Senate members. The first order of business was the financial institutions that were on the brink of collapse. The committee immediately submitted a plan that would stop the bleeding while a solution to go forward could be carved out.

## FANTASY

In the case of the auto industry the committee felt it would be best if General Motors entered into bankruptcy and renegotiate all its debt and union contracts. If need be when reorganization was accepted the Federal Government would lend them the working capital required.

The committee focused on creating jobs and developed a plan of incentives available to entrepreneurs for each additional employee added to their payroll. As part of the incentives, the government backed low interest loans to small businesses. The SBA would adopt an expedited plan that would be redacted of red tape.

Incentives where created on the same funding basis to encourage new and existing entrepreneurs to invest in new or existing businesses which will guarantee the hiring of additional employees

The committee to establish clean energy, was assigned the management of the Environmental Protection Agency.The committee was charged with selecting qualified members, whose function is for the scientific betterment to society rather than some radical ideology

History dictates that the largest deterrent to progress rests with the Environmental Protection Agency. Programs that encourage and create ingenuity, employment and independence are hampered by their archaic ways.

## FANTASY

With this renewed effort, it was deemed safe and clean to install the Keystone pipeline, establish an industry of fracking, and reduce the safeguards on coal to a financially prudent level.

By establishing these more realistic industry standards the United States would be able to provide all the energy needs for ourselves and our allies. We would not have to rely on predator countries.

In addition the opportunities for employment  would immediately repair the enemic unemployment rate we are currently facing

The goal of creating reusable energy such as solar, wind and electrically fueled vehicles would be left to the creativeness of the ambitious entrepreneurial Americans.

The advisory board recommended (and the President accepted) that any approved project will be funded only up to the extent that the principals involved have invested their own money.

The Department of Energy, concerned about the aging and outdated elements of the National Grid. Which is one of the most dangerous aspects to our security. Aside from the life threatening dangers of being without electricity, a recent terrorist attack on a station in California, increases the threat of the Grid becoming a target

## FANTASY

The committee then solicited  plans to be approved, drawn and distributed throughout the United States to upgrade the National Grid

The most qualified American engineering firms where assigned the task of specifying the responsibility of the States and coordinating the several redundant modern standards and protection from being prey to terrorism.

Each State was charged with the task of obtaining sealed bids from qualified contractors The amount of jobs this shovel-ready project could establish would in itself put the economy on solid footing.

The President campaigned on his intention to close the Guantanamo Bay Detention Camp. A committee was formed to put that into action. After a major effort by both parties in the committee it was unanimously decided that "Gitmo" was and is the best suitable location for political prisoners.

The President along with the advisory boards concluded that some of our agencies have so much power that without redundant safeguards put in place things could possibly, as in past administrations, go awry. The IRS, CIA, FBI and NSA must comply with these new programs

Surrounded by intelligent, experienced non partisan advisers The President acted on the majority opinion of their advice.

## **FANTASY**

It was concluded, for example, that the reason for the longevity of the Iraq and Afghanistan wars was that we assumed we were freeing the inhabitants from tyranny and providing them with democracy.

We did not foresee that the individual sects could not be in agreement other than with a common enemy. We did not comprehend the United States and the military could be lauded for anything other than ensuring democracy in these countries.

At the President's request an advisory board reviewed ways and means of eliminating the need for military action other than in national defense. They acknowledged that every country or sovereignty must depend on others for economic and vital needs.

The United States presented to the United Nations a proposal that would automatically trigger sanctions, embargos, and blockades for aggressive behavior, in concert with the United Nations Charter.

The sanctions would apply differently to different nations, with the intent to be severe enough for the inappropriate behavior to stop. The powers that be did not foresee the need for military response as sanctions have historically proved to be more effective.

Immigration:Through the suggestions of the advisory board and the cooperation of the chairman and members of the committee to resolve immigration issues, a multi-tiered plan was devised.

## **FANTASY**

The first tier was to be implemented immediately, the balance executed in phases over the next ten years.

Phase 1 included a counterfeit proof picture ID of every person in the United States. The purpose was to both control immigration and prevent voter fraud (which was reaching epidemic levels).

The President with the council of the advisory board met with the State Department to be sure that all of our ambassadors and Embassies throughout the world were properly protected at all times with an emphasis on the anniversary of the 9/11 terrorist attacks.

The First Lady, being an accomplished attorney, wanted to make a contribution to the new administration. Her first order of business was between herself and the President. They would organize the armies of Hollywood celebrity adoration to create a national "Peace Corps."

The Corps. will give free concerts and events such as autograph sessions in poverty stricken areas to promote academic and sex education. The higher purpose was to create ambition for a more quality lifestyle along with maintaining family values with goals in education ."

## **FANTASY**

After years of stonewalling projects and bills that would benefit the masses. Preventing income producing employment, in individual states and throughout the country, The president and the advisory committee concluded that many projects did not deploy because of partisan uncooperation.

Further examination found that the partisan negativity and delay,was the result of the influence and demands of the existing long term Majority leaders.

The Majority Leaders bow to the demands of their biggest donors. The result is the majority of Americans suffer for the few that pay for political positioning for financial benefit

In an attempt to achieve a long sought after national health plan, the advisory board met with the President. The President was convinced, that the best approach for a successful plan would be one that was Bipartisan. He gave the Senators and Congressmen a bill he intended to propose, gave them a reasonable amount of time to read, accept, reject and suggest ways to improve it.

With government shutdowns looming, the debt ceiling was next to come to the floor. It was clear to the President that the current Democratic leadership in the House and Senate did not have the same ability or desire to work on bipartisan solutions.

## **FANTASY**

In what could be the single most catalyst to work together, continue
building a Country that can be admired and counted on throughout
our borders and beyond The President decided it was time for a new
youthful approach, and requested Harry Reid and Nancy Pelosi to step
down in the interest of progress.

The President along with his advisers and new Majority Leaders
delved into the "War on Religions, Races and Sexual Orientation"

It was determined that this "Political correctness" movement is
running rampant, and it is absolutely destroying our nation.

If you say the "wrong thing" in America today, you could be
penalized, fired or even taken to court.

It is taking up the time of legislators that should be concentrating on
more important things

In the interest of what America stands for, the committee issued in the
way of a hypothetically informing statement, the following

## FANTASY

### TWO WOLVES

One evening an old Cherokee told his grandson about a
battle that goes on inside people
he said, "my son, the battle is between two wolves
Inside us all.

One is Evil. It is anger, envy, jealousy, sorrow, regret, greed
arrogance, self pity, guilt, resentment, inferiority,
lies, false pride, aging, superiority, and ego.

The other is good. It is joy, peace, love, hope, serenity,
humility, kindness, benevolence, empathy, generosity,
truth, compassion, and faith."

The grandson thought about it for a minute and then
asked his grandfather:
"which wolf wins?"

The old Cherokee simply replied:

"The one you feed."

## **FANTASY**

This is the United States of America, we all have freedom of speech and freedom of what we read and what we listen too

We have for a long time before any of the Politically Correct activists were born

We do not have to be penalized for there stupidity, we will not stand in there way, they shall not stand in ours

If you need to feed your atheist feelings go right ahead

If you need to feed your hating of Christmas feelings go right ahead

If you need to feed your religious or sexual orientation bigotry go right ahead

But, do it without raining on someone else's parade

Because of the bipartisan cooperation the administration had accomplished more than any other in the history of the United States.

Nearing the end of his tenure, President Obama was lauded throughout the entire world for his unprecedented organization of advisory boards and his ability to get the political parties to negotiate, compromise and execute as needed

## **FANTASY**

In effect he oversaw the successful launching and operation of a coalition government. These actions, and his ability as an orator and skill in concluding projects with bipartisan cooperation, created a legacy that will be hard to replicate.

President Obama had opened the barriers between minorities, reignited the spark in every human being that nothing is impossible, and created a formula of success to be followed throughout the world.

There has never been anyone that has done more positive things for their race, country and humanity.

For their efforts, Michelle and Barack Obama were awarded Nobel prizes and medals and documents of honor from all the continents of the World

## FACT

**January 7, 2009** The Justice Department began to investigate that on Election Day in 2008, two members of the New Black Panther Party for Self-Defense (NBPP) were seen and filmed standing at the entrance to a polling station in Philadelphia,

The men wore uniforms of the NBPP, stood side-by-side while obstructing the entrance, and yelled racial slurs at would-be voters.

One of the men carried a metal baton and tapped it in his hand. The incident was witnessed by lawyers and poll workers who indicated that not only did the events happen, but that potential voters turned away from the location after seeing the men.

.
None of the defendants responded to legal action and the Justice Department was set to win the case by default on May 1, 2009.

Just prior to entering the default, the Justice Department filed for a two week extension . One week later, May 15th 2009 they dropped the case against all parties except the man holding the club.

One DOJ lawyer for the case, J. Christian Adams resigned in protest. He gave testimony in response to a subpoena that the case against the remaining defendants was strong.

## **FACT**

He also echoed earlier rumors that the NAACP was involved with the decision to drop the case. Prior to his resignation, he was told to ignore the subpoenas.

The DOJ has a policy of not enforcing voting rights laws in a race neutral manner. No cases would be brought against minorities who suppressed white votes, plus other similar accusations

Christopher Coates was one of the career lawyers who had brought the case and continued to push its merits The Justice Department transferred. Mr.. Coates to South Carolina - out of the jurisdiction

In his going-away speech, he spoke about the case and read prepared remarks indicating his strong desire to see the case reopened. The case was investigated internally and remained closed

**February of 2009**The Obama administration required the director of the Census Bureau to report directly to the White House.

The prior precedent was for the Department of Commerce not to be circumvented. The census could not be  placed under any  political operatives  As creative accounting could  alter a census to politically favor one party over another

## **FACT**

**March of 2009**:**Anthony "Van" Jones** was appointed by President Obama to the newly created position of "Special Advisor for Green Jobs".  Not long after his appointment, questions began to arise concerning his socialist opinions and associations with socialist groups, comments about President Bush and Republicans, and his signing of a "911 Truth" website declaring that President Bush was involved with the terrorist attacks of 9-11

These questions plus a career of anti American rhetoric led a number of Republicans and several conservative personalities to call for his resignation or termination.  On September 6, 2009 Mr. Jones resigned from his position.

Sixty minutes had a piece on one particular Mercy ship which is a hospital that travels around the world to wherever it is needed and performs the most modern procedures to aide those in need.

This is just one example of the Humanitarian resolve of the United States. There are other Agency's, other ships and planes. There are other Doctors, Nurses. Medical assistants. There are medicine's, food and shelter prepared and ready to go anywhere in the World that they might be needed. In addition to so many  tasks of assistance the United States of America, takes on.

## **FACT**

However the radicals the ideologs the characters, this "American Anti America brigade", will only spout on what might be considered a blemish. Never to acknowledge all the good we bring to the world.

To add insult to injury there friend, our newly elected President, a man of limited experience, travels around the World to apologize for our behavior

**Summer of 2009**, A friend of President Obama's was arrested after police responded to a breaking and entering call. President Obama's friend is African American and the arresting officer is white.

Charges of racism ensued and President Obama made unsubstantiated claims about the officer's behavior. When his claims drew criticism, President Obama called for a beer summit with the arresting officer and the President's friend.

**August 4, 2009**, **Mark Lloyd** was appointed to be Associate General Counsel and Chief Diversity officer of the U.S. Federal Communications commission.

His past involvement in radio and TV and his previously stated positions on the government's role in media lead to his designation as the "Diversity Czar."

## **FACT**

Mark Lloyds appointment was controversial because of a number of comments he has made in the past concerning race and socialism. His comments are especially troubling given that he was being appointed to an office that gives him regulatory power over diversity in the broadcast market.

He has shown a marked desire to use that same authority to silence dissenting views on talk radio. He has also shown admiration for the use of media manipulation in silencing dissent for the Venezuelan takeover by Hugo Chavez.

Mark Lloyd had shown a pattern of propaganda using debunked methodology to establish an unproven basis for limiting the time and reach of opposing views

He had authored books and documents which seek to place a fee on opposing views which would then be used to support views of his ideology. He called this diversity.

He has voiced support for the socialist revolution in Venezuela and for the manipulation of media there.

He has blamed the media for discussing dissenting views about global warming and allowing an opposing view to be a legitimate idea.

## FACT

He states that this inclusion of opposing ideas represents an inability
to have a sustained intelligent conversation

**April, 2010** the investigation of the massive oil leak from a Chevron
ocean rig concluded that if the rig was built to the approved
engineered specifications, it would have been impossible for the
devastating accident to have occurred. The specifications had so many
redundant systems and controls to stop the flow of oil that this
disaster had to be the result of greed. Whether it was the owner or the
inspectors or a combination of both, the investigation should have
gone in the direction of the DOJ with criminal charges being filed on
those that  closed there eyes to the elimination of the  redundancy and
profited by it

**Jon Corzine** has been the Governor of New Jersey, a Senator from
New Jersey, and one of the heads of Goldman Sachs. In March of
2010, he took over as CEO of MF Global, a company that had already
experienced financial and regulatory problems.

During his time there, he invested in the sovereign debt of Europe by
purchasing bonds from PIIGS countries (Portugal,Italy,Greece and
Spain) after they had been downgraded. Anticipating that the
European Union would reach a deal and the value of those bonds
would increase. The rate that MF Global was required to pay on those
bonds fluctuated with MF Global's rating and that of the bonds.

## **FACT**

The amount that MF Global was leveraged combined with the sheer size of the $6.3 billion bond purchase and the continuing trouble in Europe caused MF Global to collapse in October of 2011.

As that collapse was unfolding, Mr Corzine allegedly used funds from customer segregated accounts to cover margin calls in hopes of fighting off bankruptcy, an act which is illegal. After the collapse, it was revealed that as much as $1.6 billion in customer funds was missing.

The MF Global trustees have asserted that Mr Corzine requested that those customer funds be used. This also means that Mr. Corzine committed perjury when he testified to Congress that he was unaware of the transfers or the location of the funds.

**August of, 2012**, it was reported that the Justice Department would not be pressing charges against MF Global or Jon Corzine.

This led many to speculate that the reason for the lack of charges was the close connections between Mr. Corzine , President Obama, and AG Eric Holder,as well as Mr. Corzine's past as a bundler for President Obama

## **FACT**

The Constitution, grants the President the power to appoint people with the advice and consent of the Senate, meaning that the Senate must confirm the President's appointments to the relevant offices

When the Senate is not available, or in a recess, the President can appoint people to those posts who may remain in office until they receive the Senate's confirmation or until the end of the next Senate session. These are known as recess appointments.

During the Recess of March 27, 2010 fifteen Czar appointments were made

**Craig Becker** appointed to the National Labor Relations board was the most controversial. The five member National Labor Relations Board is tasked with supervising union elections, investigating labor practices and, issuing rulings that interpret the National Labor Relations Act.

Republicans in the Senate believed that Mr. Becker's previous job as associate general counsel at the Service Employees International Union, coupled with past statements favoring unions made Mr. Becker's viewpoint biased.

## FACT

**Dr. Donald Berwick** Another recess appointment to be head of the Centers for Medicare and Medicaid Services (CMS). In this position, Dr. Berwick was not only in charge of Medicare and Medicaid, but he is also  oversaw the implementation of the 2009 health care reform legislation, which could include adding 16 million people to Medicaid.

The appointment of Dr. Berwick to this position is controversial because:

Dr. Berwick has openly advocated for redistribution of wealth through health care

Dr. Berwick has openly called for "justice in health care" according to race

Dr. Berwick has openly stated that "excellent health care is by definition redistributive"

Dr. Berwick has called for reduced care in certain areas
Such as Reduced Neonatal,Reduced Organ Transplantation
and Reduced High Tech Imaging

## FACT

**Summer of 2010**: a controversy was unfolding concerning a Mosque and community center that was to be built on grounds damaged during the 9/11 attacks.

Critics of the project cited it's name, location, leader and source of funding as indications that the mosque was intended to be a "victory mosque"

This would commemorate the victory of 9/11 for Islamic extremists. Supporters note the legal right of the owners to build on the property and state that the project is meant to build bridges between communities rather than foster mistrust.

President Obama delivered a strong defense for a proposed Muslim community center and mosque near ground zero in Manhattan, using a White House dinner celebrating Ramadan to proclaim that "as a citizen, and as President, I believe that Muslims have the same right to practice their religion as anyone else in this country."

**November 3rd 2010**. The mid term election results favoring the Republican party should have stopped the bleeding of the United States of America. The Economy should improved the prospects for American entrepreneurs.Workers should have a confidence that had been lacking for almost two years. In addition, the hope existed that the next Presidential election would bring hope and change

## **FACT**

None of the positive thoughts could manifest as Democrat Senate
Leader Harry Reid has become "the most dangerous man in the
world," "an imperial majority leader," and a "wannabe totalitarian,"
according to several headlines.

Harry Reid has been on an unprecedented power trip—from rewriting
the Constitution to fit his political needs, using the "nuclear option" to
change the Senate rules, unilaterally pushing through President
Obama's liberal appointees and judicial nominees, and circumventing
the normal checks and balances system to ram through his radical
agenda.It's unlike anything we've ever seen. And it's terrifying.

Reid's abuses of power – and the desperate and deceitful measures he
has taken to hold onto his position as Majority Leader – are nothing
short of radical, unethical and downright disturbing. He truly is the
most dangerous man for America.

In the past year, Harry Reid only allowed Republicans to vote on nine
of their proposed amendments. This type of action is not only
deplorable It prevents everything America stands for and in defiance
of our constitution

Campaign rhetoric stated "We'll put nearly half a million people to
work building wind turbines and solar panels, constructing fuel-
efficient cars and buildings, and developing the new energy
technologies that will lead to new jobs."

### FACT

Once in office the President included $90 billion in the American
Recovery and Reinvestment Act – the stimulus — to fund them.

Today, perhaps, he regrets the optimism of those heady pre-
inauguration days – especially the part about solar panels.

The failure of a number of green energy companies that received such
financing had proven to be a continuing source of embarrassment to
Obama as he sought  re-election.

For example, Beacon Power, an energy-storage company that
received a $43 million loan guaranteed from the federal government,
filed for bankruptcy in October, 2011.

Abound Solar, a solar-panel maker that received $70 million in
taxpayer funds (but had been approved by the Department of Energy
for $400 million), filed for bankruptcy in July, 2012.

Amonix  another solar panel manufacturer,closed a plant in Nevada
that had been awarded $5.9 million in stimulus money

Solyndra,, A California-based company that – once again – made
solar panels obtained $535 million,

## FACT

**August 31, 2011**, Solyndra announced it would lay off remaining workers and declare bankruptcy.  A few days later, on September 8, the FBI raided its offices in search of evidence as to whether the company filed misleading data with the government That investigation stopped there.

**Due Diligence** The money and opportunities that is wasted by not doing the proper due diligence and accountability such as, Green Energy Projects. is mind boggling. How do we the American people not have a safety net to prevent  awards of millions to billions of dollars either fraudulently or without the proper research

**March 12, 2012** In preparation for the next Presidential election the primaries began for the Republican candidate.  Mr.Gingrich making the most noise, probably knew he was going no where  He took it as far as he could to increase his speaking fee. I believe that his presence, and aggressive debating, was a determining factor in Mitt Romney's loss

**July 16, 2012**  President Obama spoke at a campaign rally in Roanoke, Virginia,In that speech, he discussed  his desire to see taxes raised on higher earners in an effort to reduce the deficit and His view was that those high earners were willing to pay more

## **FACT**

He asserted that they were aware that their businesses were successful because of the success, infrastructure, and education of others. In doing this, he used the phrase "you didn't build that"

The implication was that those businesses could not exist without the manpower and infrastructure provided by the Government.

These statements caused a great deal of controversy throughout the 2012 campaign.

Republicans seized on the statements to drive home the assertion that President Obama was hostile to business and unaware of how businesses are started in the US.

A night of the Republican National Committee in Tampa Bay, Florida was designated as "We Built It" night. In addition to the "you didn't build that" phrase,

Republicans were critical of the additional statements by President Obama that those who run successful businesses are not smarter or harder working than the rest of the country.

I was also offended by Obama's statement. I took over a company with two employees, and built that company to over 300 full time employee's

## **FACT**

Not only did I not receive any help, I built it in spite of, being hindered by laws such as "Collective Bargaining" and "The Davis Bacon Act"

**July 31, 2012**. Newsman Brian Williams interviewed Mitt Romney at the London Olympics and asked what he thought of the problems the British were having, with security, strikes, and traffic.

Romney casually answered all questions, in addition to saying it did not look like Britain was ready. All hell broke loose, He said a stupid thing in an ally country

Karl Rove, and other conservatives and Republicans said," he could have been more delicate", or, "it was a gaffe" They did not say he was misinterpreted or he meant something else, they said it was a gaffe

The truth is what he said was an off the cuff honest observation,

The point is that the media and the Democrats defend Obama's every action, The "you didn't' build that "speech" was not meant as it was taken, it was excused as "you misunderstood" Democrats and Obama do not make "gaffes"

## **FACT**

It appears to me as an Independent, in an atmosphere that is predominately Democratic, that this party never owns up to a mistake, gaffe, or a stupid statement.

They defend even the dumbest of missteps, never acknowledging the fact that maybe it could have been phrased better. How can we have bipartisanship when we are dealing with that kind of denial?

How can our body of lawmakers accomplish anything in that type of atmosphere?

Prior to the election of 2012 it was my opinion that the young people of today need to pray that Romney is their next President. That would be the catalyst to a long succession of ideal legislators. If Romney were to be elected, prosperity will again be easily achievable by those who wish to educate themselves and work toward their goals. The world will become a safer place.

The mere premise of Romney being elected will be a catalyst for hope and change. Hope will heal cabin fever and ignite spending. This should spiral into a fast and sure recovery, without the new administration even taking office.

## **FACT**

**September 23, 2012**. The Benghazi tragedy, was caused by Political Posturing. I would believe that Hillary Clinton was stuck between a rock and a hard place.

She could not defy Obama by rejecting the current stance on the Arab revolt.

She had no choice but to accept it. either way, when she let Obama politically seduce her, she was a goner.

The Benghazi disgrace in Libya was upon her. She may not have pulled the trigger, but she put herself in a position where there was nothing she could do but accept the phony rhetoric and cover up of the administration.

The fact that the white House was engaged in campaigning, and not protecting was incompetence. They did not have there eye on the ball.

Because of that and the Secretary of State, who is the person to handle that 3 A.M. call not coming to there aide  four Americans lost there lives and countless family, friends, loved ones and Americans lost there pride

## **FACT**

She was in that position because she played politics and moved the wrong chess piece; therefore, we cannot let her be President of our country now, when there is no room for any wrong moves.

The Benghazi call came in at 3pm not 3 am and there was no one home

**November, 2012** The Election is over and President Obama remains in office for four more years. How is this possible with all the scandals, lies, incompetence and political back stabbing?

It is possible because the Chicago-based campaign machine is a lot smarter than we thought. They have essentially unionized the middle to lower income voters. Their purpose is to perpetuate the Democratic party, to allow it to remain in control, forever. These people have better knowledge of the tools of communication available today, and they know how to use them.

This consortium calculated the areas of the country that if electorally lost might be decisive in the election. They calculated the ethnic, female, union, Democratic and Republican votes. The only thing they had to do was to make sure the people got to the polls, and they did.

## **FACT**

They picked them up, drove them to the polls, made sure they voted, gave them coffee and donuts, drove them home. Just in case that was not enough, they recalled the deceased, cloned them and brought them to the polls as well (several times).

Four more years, weak economy, absent foreign policy, stalemated legislators. Four more years of Harry Reid's almost senile vitriol, four more years of hiding proposed bills not to his liking.

Four more years of Nancy Pelosi  contrived republican wars on women, children, race, poor and whatever is popular at the time And let us not forget, if your not sure who is at fault, Bush the younger has broad shoulders.

Four more years of you did not build that so redistribute your earnings to those who do not want to work

The people in the box seats such as the Michael Moore's and the Bill Maher's will criticize capitalism and applaud redistribution of wealth. But, with a slight caveat: not their money and not their talent.

There are some very well educated holders of major academic awards that are in bed with this group. The only way I can understand it is they are good at retaining and testing. But  the element of common sense , is missing .

## FACT

Which leads me to Obama again. The words used regarding him are "very smart guy," "very eloquent."!  On what basis?  That he was admitted to Harvard? That he can read a teleprompter? If he were a smart guy, he would get things done, with give and take not stonewalling. Smart is not the criteria, the combination of common sense and smart is

Experience is the catalyst for common sense

The real problem is how we will ever get back to America, the home of the free and the brave, where every non-entitled parent tells their children they can be whatever they set their mind to, as long as they work for it.

The amount of people that understand what is going on is not enough to win an election. How can a non entitlement candidate today going to convince the people that get perpetual unemployment, perpetual food stamps, and perpetual aide to vote for them ?

That is why this administration can create their own numbers, statements, and lies. There is nothing that can be done about it. You can stand up and say "you are lying" but who is going to listen? Not the majority that has been bought by entitlements!

## **<u>FACT</u>**

In order to criticize the current leadership or party, you have to walk on egg shells. Any statement could be interpreted as "Racist". If you can get past that label, you have the wrath of the most powerful Government Agencies in the United States investigating you.

I fear that there is nothing positive that will come from any of this. If we can ever recover and get back to basics, we will see at minimum Greece-like mob scenes and, not so unrealistic, a civil war.

Glen Beck pegged it immediately. But his dramatic approach scared people away.

Mark Levin's approach was too intellectual.

Rush Limbough's too emotional.

Any other criticism of the Obama administration is labeled "Racial."

There is one pundit voice out there that is motivated by intellect and common sense, and presented with soft spoken facts that cannot be denied: "Charles Krauthammer"

## FACT

**October 1, 2013** The federal government shut down over a fiscal stalemate because of bipartisanship.The Democrats blamed the Republicans.

The House  GOP made several offers of compromise to prevent  the shutdown  The only thing the republicans wanted was a smithering of fiscal responsibility. Senate Democrats and the White House firmly rejected each bill.

In Washington DC Federal parks were barricaded to demonstrate its closure. The White House stopped all tours as there were no employees to administer them. The administration stated that the Republicans where causing the lay offs and firing of hundreds of thousands of government employee's

In the end the Republicans caved and the deal to reopen the government did virtually nothing to alter the out of control fiscal responsibility

In 2014 as facts are starting to come to the surface ,It seems the Government shutdown caused one employee to lose his job.

Everything was just smoke and mirrors to make the Republicans the bad guys. Without any concern for people and schools that planned trips to the Whitehouse a year or more prior

## FACT

**AFFORDABLE CARE ACT**

From the time Nancy Pelosi advocated to 'just sign it, read it later,' the 2,471 page affordable Obama care mandate has been nothing less than a disaster.

This is a debacle of incompetence, ineptness and an embarrassing disgrace. From the refusal of the White House and majority leaders to negotiate a bipartisan bill, the hiring of a non-American software company with a no-bid contract, the inability to have a realistic budget set with contingencies, to having an inexperienced administrator oversee its implementation, the birth and delivery of this program has failed.

The only thing good about it is the concept

The Affordable Care Act's federal enrollment website was supposed to be the easy part of the law's rollout. During its construction, the system was repeatedly compared to sites like Travelocity and Match.com, where millions of users can simultaneously navigate a complex individualized shopping experience.

## FACT

**July,2013** The administration changed one more of the over fifty illegal law changes, larger employers would not be required to offer health insurance to their workers until 2015. The decision came in reaction to pressure from the business community.

The month of January 2014 saw lawmakers and most staffers enter ObamaCare's new insurance exchanges, but this shift did not come without controversy.

The first firestorm came in the summer when the administration ruled that members and aides can continue receiving a generous employer health care subsidy despite moving out of the Federal Employee Health Benefits Plan.

Conflict reared its head again when news broke that lawmakers could keep their aides off of the exchanges by deeming them "official staff" instead of "official office."

Some pro-Obama Care offices later regretted choices to shift workers on the exchanges, citing higher costs for older staffers.

## **FACT**

Aides also encountered problems enrolling in the District of Columbia's new marketplace, and received notices to confirm their sign-ups in person rather than online.

As I write in the beginning of March 2014, we have seen a resurgence of consumer interest with the enrollment deadline approaching. The administration said HealthCare.gov received 1.5 million visits on Wednesday, March 2, 2014

However it too comes with a caveat: The administration has yet to announce how many consumers actually closed the deal by paying their first month's premium.

Some independent estimates are that as many as 10 percent to 20 percent have not paid, which would bring the total enrollment to between 5 million and 6 million people.

Finally, a positive note to bring to light. The one person that could assure us of its success, Former House Democratic leader Nancy Pelosi of California, said in a statement:

"Republicans should abandon their reckless pursuit of new milestones in the number of votes to repeal or undermine this historic law."

## FACT

The amount of people that have enrolled and paid in the health care bill, will not be known while this administration is in office. They have insured that and eliminated any accountability by guaranteeing the insurance companies a bailout for any losses

ERIC HOLDER

"Fast and Furious" gun-walking program – Attorney General Eric Holder was cited for contempt of Congress in a dispute over documents the panel sought in the "Fast and Furious" investigation.

A strong call for his resignation loomed. His defiance in the face of the House contempt citation indicates Holder won't voluntarily step down unless pressured to do so by Obama, who has steadfastly maintained confidence in him.

The question will be whether Holder is a liability for the President or an ally. If the multiple controversies (IRS targeting, Benghazi, reporters phone records) continue to dominate the political discussion, one would think that Obama would decide a drastic gesture is needed to try to move past a climate of crises. However, nothing at this point suggests that is imminent or under consideration or that the administration concerns itself with a crisis climate.

## **FACT**

Holder's bad advice began almost immediately after Obama took office. Holder proclaimed he will "work to restore the credibility of a department badly shaken by allegations of improper political interference. Law enforcement decisions and personal actions must be untainted by partisanship."

From the moment he uttered those words to this very day, Eric Holder's tenure as Attorney General has been marred by controversy and obstruction. But his failures as a leader began long before operation Fast and Furious made national headlines.

In 2009 (as noted prior) he provoked a political firestorm by withdrawing a lawsuit against the New Black Panther Party for violations of the Voting Rights Act, over the objections of six career lawyers at the Justice Department.

And then there was Holder's decision to sue the state of Arizona over its popular immigration law, above the objections of three Arizona Democrats engaged in tough reelection fights (two of whom lost their seats).

## **FACT**

In 2010, the Department Of Justice obtained phone records, e-mails and security badge tracking of a Fox News correspondent who reported on information that was supposed to be classified intelligence about North Korea. Holder claimed to congress that he had nothing to do with obtaining the search warrants.

Justice Department officials contradicted Holder saying that he took part in "discussions" about seeking the search warrant.

President Barrack Obama ordered Holder to review government practices in investigating leaks of secret information. This meant Holder was investigating himself.

The next avoidable firestorm came with Holder's decision to release classified Justice Department memos on the CIA terrorist interrogation program and reopen criminal investigations into the conduct of CIA interrogators.

Before his decision to reopen the cases, Holder did not read detailed memos that (career) prosecutors drafted and placed in files to explain their decision to decline prosecutions. If he had bothered to do so, he could have predicted the eventual outcome.

## **FACT**

The special prosecutor he appointed came to the same conclusion as the career prosecutors under the Bush administration and found no criminal wrongdoing by the CIA officials involved in the agency's rendition, Detention and Interrogation program. After two years of wasted resources and needless controversy, Holder came up empty.

Then came Holder's order to read Christmas Day bomber Umar Farouk Abdulmutallab a Miranda warning after just 50 minutes of questioning – an order the Attorney General gave without even consulting chief intelligence or national security officials.

Holder's administration colleagues were forced to argue (implausibly) that Miranda was really not an impediment to effective interrogation – only to have Holder undercut them a few months later when he admitted that this was not true. He asked Congress to fix the Miranda law to allow longer interrogations.

Not only did Holder's Miranda decision cost America valuable intelligence, the ensuing controversy helped propel Scott Brown to victory in the Massachusetts Senate race, costing Obama his filibuster-proof majority in the Senate. According to Brown's chief strategist, internal polls showed the treatment of enemy combatants was a more potent issue in the election than was health care.

## **FACT**

Then there was Holder's catastrophic attempt to try Khalid Sheikh
Mohammed and the other 9/11 plotters in federal court in New York
City. Holder made the decision alone, at 1 a.m., while eating Chips
Ahoy cookies at his kitchen table.

He did so without first consulting New York officials, who responded
with outrage, as did the general public. In the face of the bipartisan
backlash, the administration was forced to backtrack, and it soon
announced the resumption of military commission trials at
Guantanamo for Mohammed and other terrorists.

This only scratches the surface of ill-fated Holder initiatives. Many of
these debacles stem from Holder's failure to do due diligence.

He failed to consult the intelligence community before giving the
Christmas bomber a Miranda warning;

He failed to read the memos in which career prosecutors explained
why CIA prosecutions were a legal dead end;

He failed to consult New York officials about trying Mohammed in
their city

## **FACT**

He failed to conduct even a cursory review before pushing Obama to announce the closure of Guantanamo

He failed to read the Arizona immigration law before publicly opposing it.

One failure is a mistake. This many is either gross incompetence or by design. Given his record of stumbling into one foreseeable and avoidable controversy after another, it is amazing Holder is still at his post.

President Obama stated that he has "complete confidence" in Attorney General Eric Holder.

That's good news for Republicans. Pick almost any unnecessary, losing battle in Obama's first term and his hapless Attorney General is at the center of it. If not for the fact that so many of Holder's decisions harm national security, he would be a political dream come true for the GOP – delivering up reliably disastrous controversies for the President every few months.

When you logically review this report it is easy to question just what Eric Holder knows or holds over Obama's head that prevents him from taking the obvious appropriate action to fire Holder immediately.

## **FACT**

Any lawyer who fails to conduct thorough due diligence is a danger to his clients and in this case, a nation. Many are of the opinion that Mr. Holder is Mr. Obama's albatross. I think not. This administration appears to tell untruths easily and without regard to repercussions. Mr. Holder is not an albatross, but a partner in deceit.

**SCANDAL SUMMARY**

1.. The IRS targets Obama's enemies.

The IRS targeted conservative and pro-Israel groups prior to the 2012 election. Questions are being raised about why this occurred, who ordered it, whether there was any White House involvement and whether there was an initial effort to hide who knew about the targeting and when.

2. Benghazi. This is actually three scandals in one.

A. The failure of the administration to protect the Benghazi Embassy.

B. The changes made to the talking points in order to suggest the attack was motivated by an anti-Muslim video.

## **FACT**

C. The refusal of the White House to say what President Obama did the night of the attack.

3. Spying on the Associated Press.

The Justice Department performed a massive cull of AP reporters' phone records as part of a leak investigation.

4. Rosen-gate.

The Justice Department suggested that Fox News reporter James Rosen is a criminal for reporting about classified information, and subsequently monitored his phones and emails.

5. Potential Holder perjury number one

Attorney General Eric Holder told Congress he had never been associated with "potential prosecution" of a journalist for perjury when in fact he signed the affidavit that termed Rosen a potential criminal.

6. The ATF "Fast and Furious" scheme.

## FACT

7. Potential Holder perjury  number two

Holder told Congress in May 2011 that he had just recently heard about the Fast and Furious gun walking scheme when there is evidence he may have known much earlier.

8. Sebelius demands payment.

HHS Secretary Kathleen Sebelius solicited donations from companies HHS might regulate. The money would be used to help her sign up uninsured Americans for ObamaCare.

9. The Pigford scandal.

An Agriculture Department effort that started as an attempt to compensate black farmers who had been discriminated against by the agency evolved into a gravy train delivering several billion dollars in cash to thousands of additional minority and female farmers who probably didn't face discrimination.

## FACT

10. GSA gone wild.

In 2010 the General Services Administration held an $823,000 training conference in Las Vegas, featuring a clown and a mind reader. This resulted in the resignation of the GSA administrator.

11. Veterans Affairs in Disney World.

The agency wasted more than $6 million on two conferences in Orlando. An assistant secretary was fired.

12. Sebelius violates the Hatch Act.

A U.S. special counsel determined that Kathleen Sebelius violated the Hatch Act when she made "extemporaneous partisan remarks" during a speech in her official capacity last year. During the remarks, Sebelius called for the election of the Democratic candidate for governor of North Carolina.

13. Solyndra,

Republicans charged the Obama administration funded and promoted its poster boy for green energy despite warning signs the company was headed for bankruptcy

THE UNRAVELING OF AMERICA
THE OBAMA ADMINISTRATION
A TRILOGY IN 'F'

## FACT

The administration also allegedly pressed Solyndra to delay layoff announcements until after the 2010 midterm elections.

14. AKA Lisa Jackson.

Former EPA Administrator Lisa Jackson used the name "Richard Windsor" when corresponding by email with other government officials, drawing charges she was trying to evade scrutiny.

.

15. Waging war all by myself.

Obama may have violated the Constitution and both the letter and the spirit of the War Powers Resolution by attacking Libya without Congressional approval.

16. Biden bullies the press.

Vice President Biden's office has repeatedly interfered with coverage, including forcing a reporter to wait in a closet, making a reporter delete photos, and editing pool reports.

17. The administration paid millions to the former firm of then-White House adviser David Axelrod

## FACT

Mr Axelrod's firm, AKPD Message and Media, was paid to promote passage of ObamaCare. Some questioned whether the firm was hired to help pay Axelrod $2 million AKPD owed him.

18. Sestak, we'll take care of you.

Former White House Chief of Staff Rahm Emanuel used Bill Clinton as an intermediary to probe whether former Rep. Joe Sestak (Dem.-PA) would accept a prominent, unpaid White House advisory position in exchange for dropping out of the 2010 primary against former Sen. Arlen Specter (Dem.-PA).

19. I'll pass my own laws.

Obama has repeatedly been accused of making end runs around Congress by deciding which laws to enforce, including the decision not to deport illegal immigrants who may have been allowed to stay in the United States had Congress passed the "Dream Act."

20. The hacking of Sheryl Atkinson's computer.

It's not clear who hacked the CBS reporter's computer as she investigated the Benghazi scandal, but the Obama administration and its allies had both the motive and the means to do it.

## FACT

21. An American Political Prisoner.

The sudden decision to arrest Nakoula Basseley Nakoula on unrelated charges after protests in the Arab world over his anti-Muslim video is an extraordinarily suspicious coincidence. "We're going to go out and we're going to prosecute the person that made that video," Hillary Clinton allegedly told the father of one of the ex-SEALs killed in Banghazi.
.

22. Get rid of inconvenient IG's.

Inspector General  for the Corporation for National and Community Services Gerald Walpin was fired in 2009 as he fought wasteful spending and investigated a friend of Obama's, Sacramento Mayor and former NBA player Kevin Johnson. The White House says Walpin was incompetent.

23. Influence peddling.

An investigation is underway of Alejandro Mayorkas, director of the U.S. Citizenship and Immigration Services, who has been nominated by Obama for the number two post at the Department of Homeland Security.

## **FACT**

Mayorkas may have used his position to unfairly obtain U.S. visas for foreign investors in a company run by Hillary Clinton's brother, Anthony Rodman.

On April 12, 2014, the midterm elections are approaching. The Democrats were feeling weak, the Republicans strong, and neither one could afford to be stagnant.

The Democrats have put forth their campaign agenda, as of today. Women, voter identification, statistics, torture, if all else fails. The stage is being set for "Race.Baiting""

Women: Disparity in pay. What happened in the past five-plus years? Not only was the issue not brought up, but the very people who are bringing it to the surface now are the same ones that practice this disparity.

Voter Identification: Why are the Democrats so afraid of identifying qualified voters? Could it be that there have been massive, proven situations of deceased and duplicity voting? Why are they sending out "Race" provocateurs to sell this position?

## **FACT**

**CREATIVE STATISTICS:**

Over the past five-plus years, we have dealt with the unemployment statistics, economy statistics, health care statistics and more.

When I was about 18 years old I became aware of cancer and how it was terminal with no cure. Traveling to work every day by bus and train, I read the newspaper. There was an article. One of the major causes of cancer was cranberry sauce. It was not part of my diet but what I intuited was that we are heading toward finding out how to prevent it.

A week later I read another article on a cancer-causing food, and many more in the subsequent months. After a while it was apparent that the only way to avoid cancer was to not eat, or ignore the barrage of warnings. I chose to ignore them.

Today, we have informative advertisements. More people have lost more weight on this diet than any other. More people have met their spouse through this website than any other. In a study it was found that this medicine cures better than any other. It goes on and on.

## **FACT**

There is no proof of what they are saying, and if you want proof they will do a study group to create the outcome they desire. It is called creative statistics, the same technique politicians use to benefit their position.

"Creative Statistics" require a pen, a phone, and a spreadsheet

My point is we have suffered in our comfort, expense, employment and entrepreneurship by the deployment of these erroneous studies.

They are not real. If coal or oil pollutes, engineer a way to safeguard us. If the erogenous African black widow spiders are an endangered species tell us what happens if they disappear. If global warming is real, execute a legitimate study offering real consequences and possible solutions.

The progress of correcting a stalled economy is thwarted by idealistic theories that have no teeth in the facts.

The Affordable Care Act proponents are stating that 7.1 million people have signed up. That number will increase until after the midterm elections.

## **FACT**

Rand however published a full report. It indicates that ObamaCare's exchanges only enrolled 1.4 million previously uninsured individuals. The report contains a substantial margin of error, due to the study's small sample size. Rand's figures do not take into account the last few weeks of the ObamaCare open enrollment period, creating a margin of error of 700,000. The probability is that the actual number is between 700,000 and 2.1 million previously uninsured enrollees

What ever happened to good old common sense? How can people live with a double standard and convince themselves that it is okay?

Doesn't everyone think about a situation and think 'how would I feel if I was on the other side?'

To the people who came out with opinions on how terrible water boarding is and how we the United States of America do not condone torture, shame on you.

Please tell me what you would you do if the killers of 3 million innocent Americans - these radical terrorists - were ready to continue their reign of terror on your watch.

## **FACT**

.

What if it were your house that was next, or your child or school, or the place where someone dear to you would lose their life? What if your child was kidnapped and a terrorist knew where that child was being held?

Would you say the Geneva Convention dictates that you have to tell me? Or would you not only water board the terrorist, you would properly cut off each finger one at a time?

Let's stop this hypocritical nonsense and get back to basics. People, countries, and terrorists who do not like us are jealous of what we built. Jealous of our place in the World, Jealous of humanitarian and military assistance,Jealous of our effort to preserve democracy.

Are we going to satisfy them by tearing it down?

Stop pointing fingers. Let's move forward, we are smart enough to figure out the solutions, we are smart enough not to let one person block legislature to improve care for our Veterans..

Resolve the problems, let another body of investigation lay the blame if necessary

## FACT

Race:  Now we come to the really tough one, how do you deal with this prickly issue? You are trying to tell the Attorney General that he is preventing investigations from going forward because he is not cooperating.

His response: "you're a racist."

You tell the President that there is a disparity in the response between one group committing a crime on another. "You are racist."

You tell Harry Reid or Nancy Pelosi that the President's plan is not working. Not only are you a "racist" you are also a liar.

It's very hard to deal with this kind of camouflage. We all acknowledge the poor treatment that was bestowed upon people of color. We do not ever want to be on the side of being accused of something we sternly do not condone.

Mr. Holder you are a highly educated, well mannered, eloquent gentleman. That is what we see, not your color. If we saw your color we would be adding respect and acknowledgment for getting to the position you are in, a task that has been  much more difficult for people of color

## **<u>FACT</u>**

That being said, you are being scrutinized for the blatant incompetent and disrespectful handling of the highest law enforcement position in the United States of America.

Do not disrespect your race to cover up your ideology and incompetence.

May 24th, 2014

As each day goes by new scandals reach into other areas of government. The prior scandals become more apparent. The whistleblowers begin to emerge. The foreign powers delve deeper into testing our metal. The phone at the Whitehouse keeps ringing No one answers.

One of the most interesting things to me is the mindset of some of these politicians. Benghazi was a disgrace and people lost loved ones Anyone with common sense knows it was incompetence, smothered with cover up

Enough proof is starting to emerge where it necessitates investigation. There has to be accountability in everything or nothing will ever be corrected.

## FACT

While a bipartisan committee is being formed to investigate "Benghazi"

Evidence of the outright lies attributed to the government shutdown starts to emerge

There are documents appearing proving that the IRS targeting of political opponents came directly from the White House

The V A scandal comes to light. This is not the result of this administration, it is the result of many, the result of big government the result of non business experienced leaders acting out the peter principle, being incompetent in the roles they were given as political perks

Now exposed the question is who and how to piece it back together, another politician? lawyer?.

A team is needed to organize and professionally manage a tribute to those that kept us here to now. The team needs business experienced leaders and medically experienced hospital administrators

Even better, privatize all existing V A hospitals. Issue a Carte Blanche all inclusive medical card,to be used anywhere, for every returning Vet

## **FACT**

Some loyalists claim that all this investigating is for political posturing, others Profess it stems from racist motivation..

While the racist rhetoric is magnifying in the political arena, there are no facts to substantiate those claims. This type of Race Baiting could cause a severely backwards turn in the enormous progress of the past and future

No one admits that we elected a man with no experience in anything other than radical ideology to be the most powerful man in the world, and commander in chief of 300 million people and all that governs them.

Is it possible that they all believe that we are too big to fail? There is not enough time left for political posturing, political motivation, ideology, financial irresponsibility and decision making that is not fueled by common sense..

I do not think any logic minded American wants to see us have boots on the ground anywhere, ever. But we do not want to diminish who we are and what we have

## FACT

There are people and countries that do not like us. They would not like us no matter what we would do.

Because, up to now we were the number one superpower.

That by itself is the trigger, as jealousy is the most afflicting disease of Human Beings. In every Country, every Religion, every age group and every Gender

The United States was the strongest economy in the World, not for long.

The United States  was the best militarily equipped and  prepared in the World, not for long.

The United States was respected by its ally's, not any more

The United States was feared by it's current and potential enemies, not any more

The future is bleak and unless everyone steps up to the plate, takes an interest. And votes there mind, it will not get better.

## WE ARE NOT TO BIG TO FAIL

We are not to small to prevent any qualified American to lead us back to our roots. No matter there Color, Religion, or Gender

## **FUTURE**

The possibility of repairing the damage that has been done is not
probable but of course possible.

The "Teflon President" will complete his term. The amount of
additional damage is yet to be determined. The reason for the damage,
by design or ideology, is also still to be determined.

Mr. Obama and the Chicago consortium will conclude the past eight
years with  net worth's way in excess of when they began. A net
worth you can be sure will not be redistributed.

Harry Reid has amassed his own ten million dollar net worth as a
public employee all his life. And members of his family have become
wealthy from unknown sources.

The foreign powers that would like to see harm come to the United
States have been (and until there is change will continue to be)
emboldened.

The possibility of recovery rests with the next leader of our country.
Never before was it this important to have a strong leader that
believes, respects and will administer the Laws of the Constitution of
the United States.

## **FUTURE**

A leader that understands you cannot threaten  something that you do
not intend to implement.

You cannot warn a country not to cross a red line and not implement a
consequence.

A leader should not  state that Islam has a right to open a Mosque at
Ground Zero and practice their right of freedom of religion.

Then, contradict himself  and undermine the foundation of our
country by allowing anti-religious groups to control who and how we
practice our religions.

A leader that will respect an order of Catholic Nuns or any other non
violent religious institiutions and not take them to task for practicing
their religion.

A leader that does not pick and choose a law as it suits him.

A leader that would have the good sense not to legalize a proven
addictive  gateway drug.

A leader that understands and implements the proper education to our
children so that we can compete on the world stage.

## **<u>FUTURE</u>**

A leader that understands we must educate all of our children to understand the Constitution, understand our laws, understand the reasoning, and teach them the importance or if necessary the mandating of their vote.

A leader that will appoint educators to institute sample government elections for school issues that they will understand.

A leader that institutes classes to encourage, teach and promote future bipartisan legislators.

A leader that will aid in the education that life itself is predicated on earning your own way.

A leader that will present laws to Congress ensuring that when there is a survey, trial, study group, or test, the playing field has been fairly analyzed.

A leader that will get enough opinions on whether a particular endangered species is in fact more important than our national security and lifestyle.

A leader that will use his phone and pen for his family and not as a bully.

## FUTURE

A leader that will not try to prevent the progress of ingenuity to protect his own agenda, such as fracking, keystone pipelines, voter fraud or just a guitar manufacturer.

A leader that wants more out of his legacy than the two-to-three steps leading to a campaign speech platform.

If we are able to avoid ultimate collapse, it's going to take a moral awakening and renewed constitutional respect, not only by politicians but by all the American people.

"Let us not seek the Republican answer or the Democratic answer,but the right answer. Let us not seek to fix the blame for the past. Let us accept our own responsibility for the future"

John F. Kennedy

**"United we stand, divided we fall."**

www.ingramcontent.com/pod-product-compliance
Lightning Source LLC
Chambersburg PA
CBHW060206290526
45789CB00003B/1177